HEY
Carter!®
BOOKS

I0133053

Fros, Braids, Fades, & Waves

A Celebration of Black Boy Hairstyles

Written by
Thomishia Booker

Illustrated by
Starvos Pierce

For my SONshine.

Published in the USA by Hey Carter! Books 2022
www.heycarterbooks.com

My fro is poppin!
I love the way it glistens in the sun.

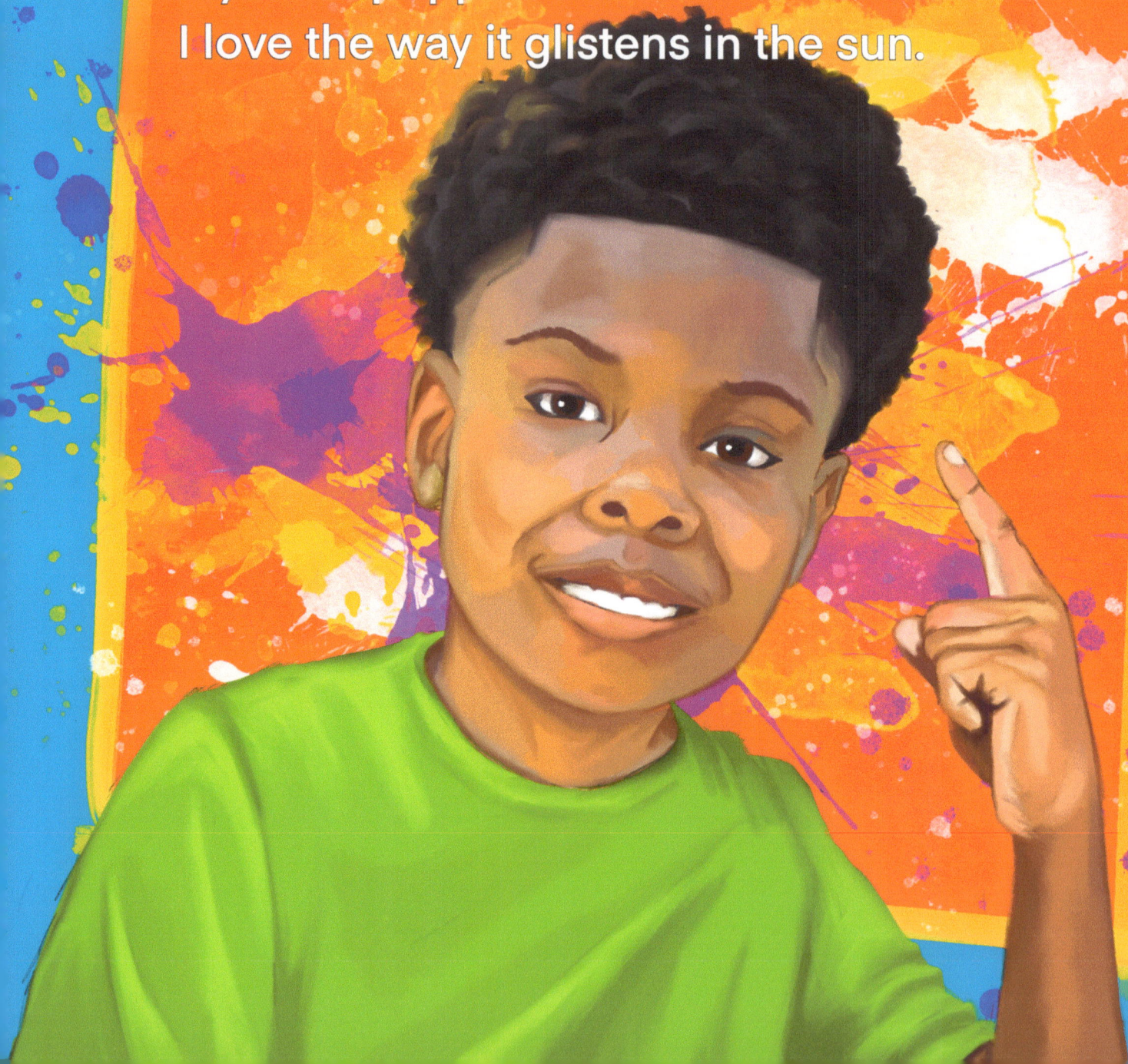

Switching up my hair from a fro to a fade is always so much fun.

A visit to the barbershop to get a lineup always makes me feel brand new.
The way I wear my hair shouldn't matter to you.

My braids swing left and right.
I love everything about my hair.
Looking this handsome and being this cool
is so unfair.

When I wear my mohawk with flames on the side, I feel so fly.
You can't touch my hair so please do not try.

My locs are bangin!
I have the hair of a warrior so powerful and strong.
I can wear my hair in any style.
Short and wavy or curly and long.

I put my durag on at night to make my waves come alive.

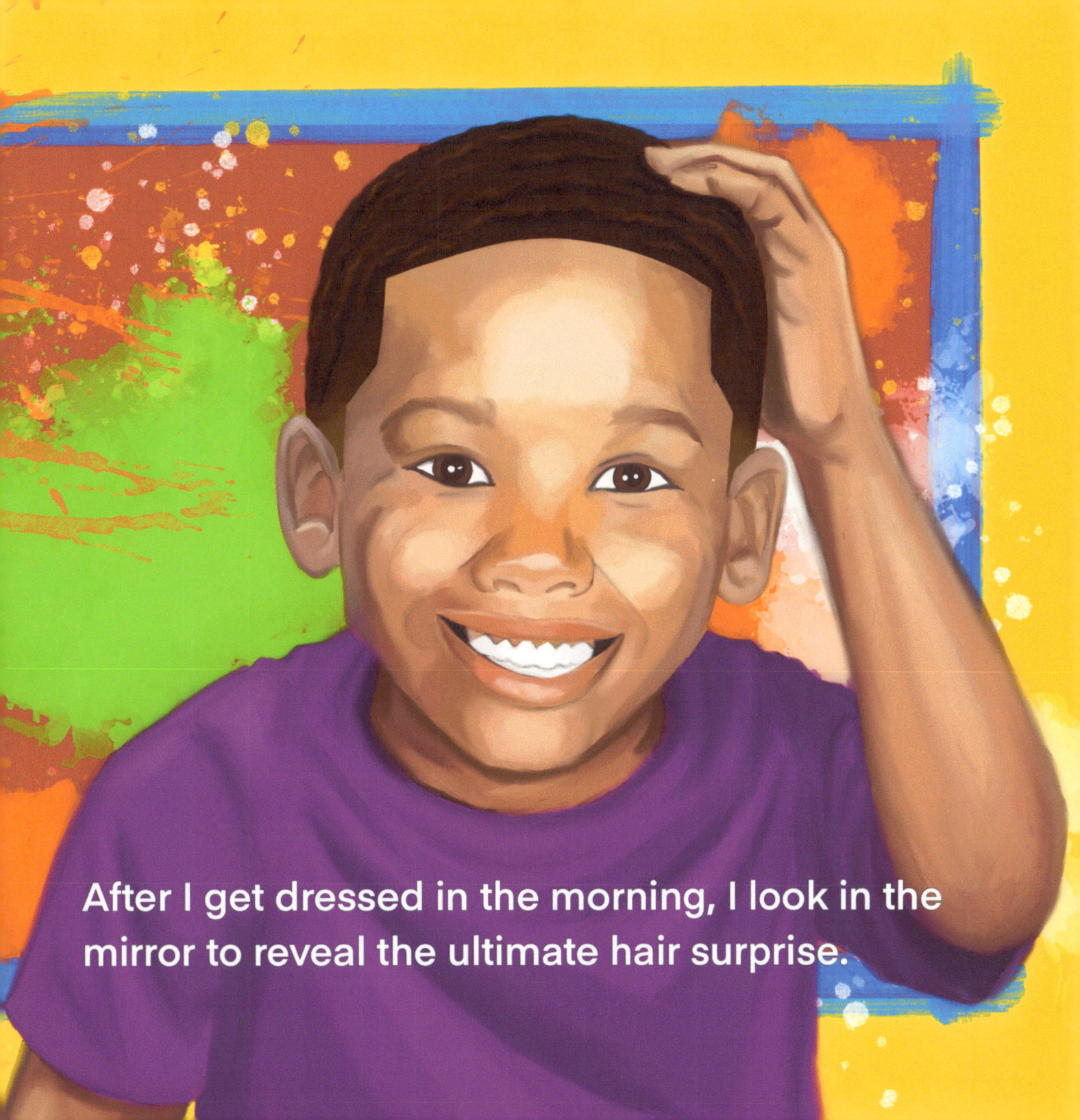

After I get dressed in the morning, I look in the mirror to reveal the ultimate hair surprise.

My curls make a statement.
They are so bold and oh so free.
Sometimes I don't do anything to my hair.
I just wake up and let it be.

During the summer I get my hair cut really low.
I don't have to do much to it when I wear it like this.
I can just get up and go.

My fade is on point!
Name any style and I can rock it.
I keep my hair looking good with a brush
inside my left pocket.

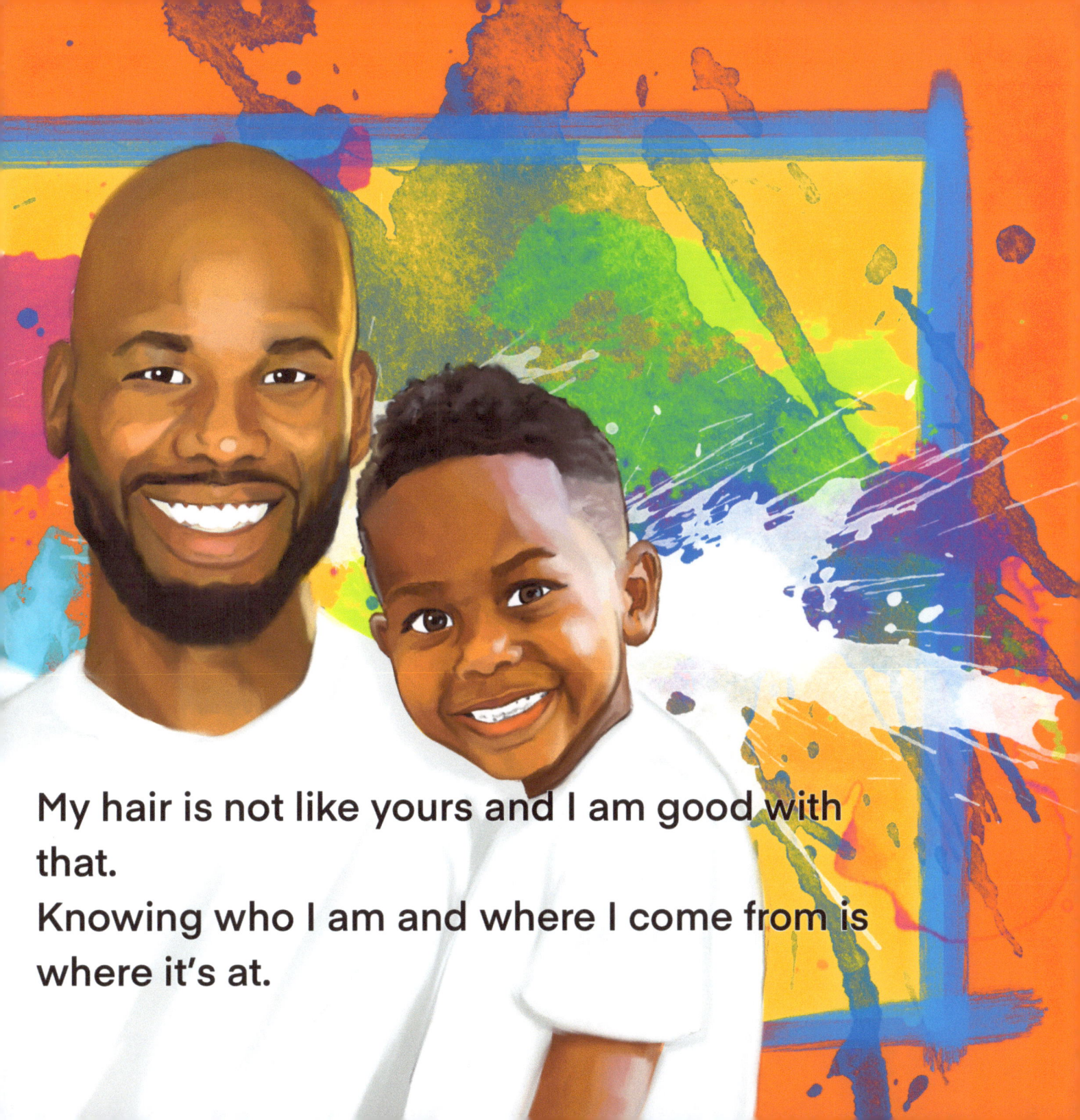

My hair is not like yours and I am good with that.
Knowing who I am and where I come from is where it's at.

HISTORY

STRENGTH

My hair tells a story.
There is no one else in this world who looks just like me.
I take pride in my hair and I am exactly who I want to be.

Thomishia Booker is a celebrated self-published children's book author from East Side San Jose, California. She is the author of the Hey Carter! Children's Book Series which has been recognized by the Black Caucus American Library Association and the American Library Association. Her book Brown Boy Joy was featured on the Netflix original series Bookmarks: Celebrating Black Voices where she was the only self-published author featured on the show. She is passionate about changing false narratives that exist for Black children and showing the world "Happy Black children living their happy Black lives." Thomishia is a licensed therapist, wife, and mother of two.

Starvos is a professional painter and illustrator from New Orleans, LA. Discovering his gift and passion for art at an early age, he has created art ever since he first learned to use a pencil. His work includes original pieces, commissioned artwork, private portraiture for celebrities, athletes, and collectors, book illustrations and covers, logos, live painting, concept art, and everything in between. His current technique is based on formal and self guided training in acrylics translated to the world of digital paint. He holds two degrees in theology and is always looking to let God speak in and through his work. Starvos currently resides in Baton Rouge, LA with his wife and two kids.

www.ingramcontent.com/pod-product-compliance
Lightning Source LLC
LaVergne TN
LVHW072110070426
835509LV00002B/103